CONTENTS

1. Cato vs Clouseau — 2
2. Take a Look — 4
3. Gorgeous George — 6
4. Shark Soup — 8
5. Brown Paper Cowboy — 10
6. Over and Over — 12
7. I've Got a Groove — 14
8. Fourth Street — 16
9. Let the Good Times Roll — 18
10. Blue Onions — 20

Scan QR code to hear the tunes and for the play-along tracks.

ISBN 97-8 1911359-13-5
Published by EVC Music Publications Ltd
© 2017 EVC Music Publications Ltd
All Rights Reserved. Unauthorised reproduction of any part of this publication by any means including photocopying is prohibited by law.

CATO VS CLOUSEAU

Sam Wedgwood

Medium swing ♩ = 120

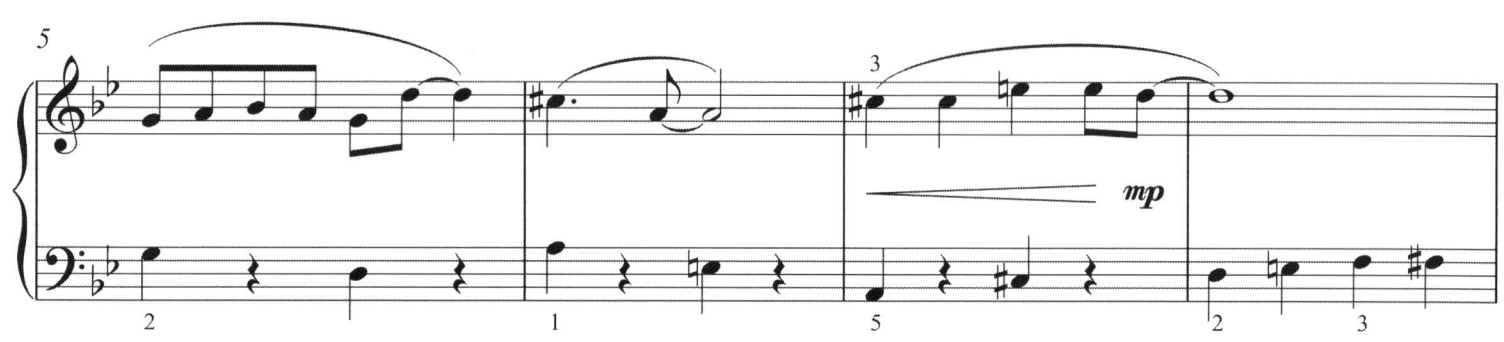

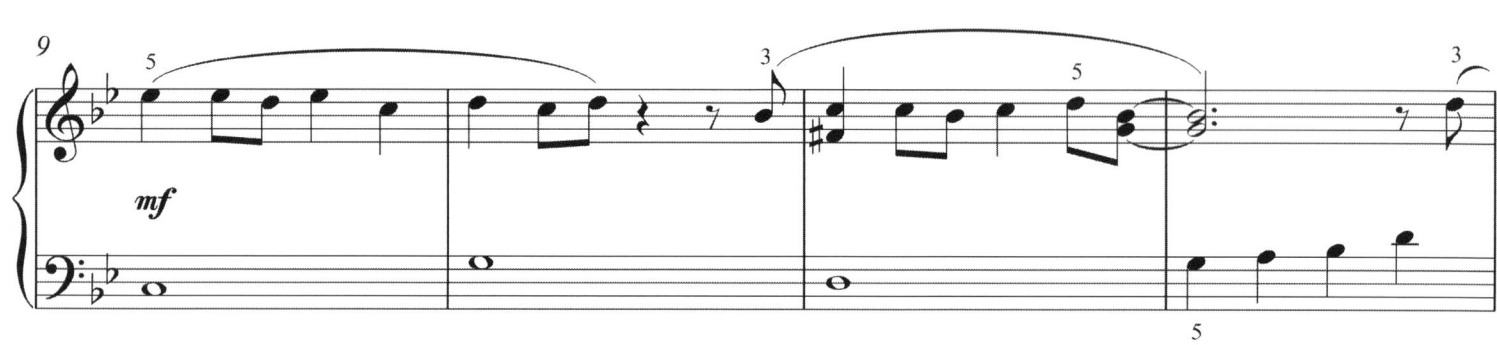

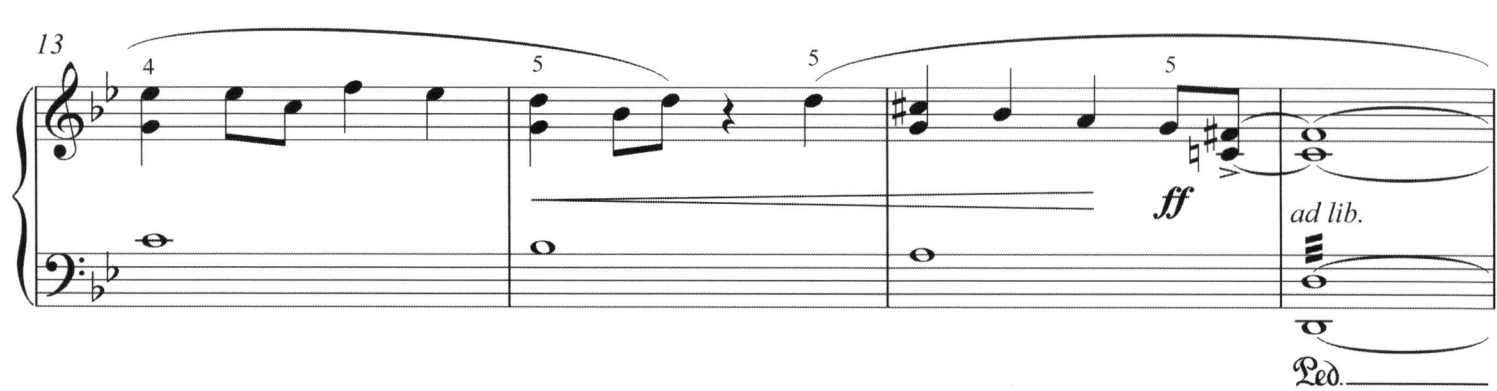

Copyright © 2017 EVC Music Publications Ltd EVC034

TAKE A LOOK

Sam Wedgwood

Copyright © 2017 EVC Music Publications Ltd EVC034

GORGEOUS GEORGE

Sam Wedgwood

Swing in a boystrous manner ♩ = 112

poco rall.
a tempo
mp
sfz
p
ad lib.
sfz
pp
Play a cluster
of notes
8vb

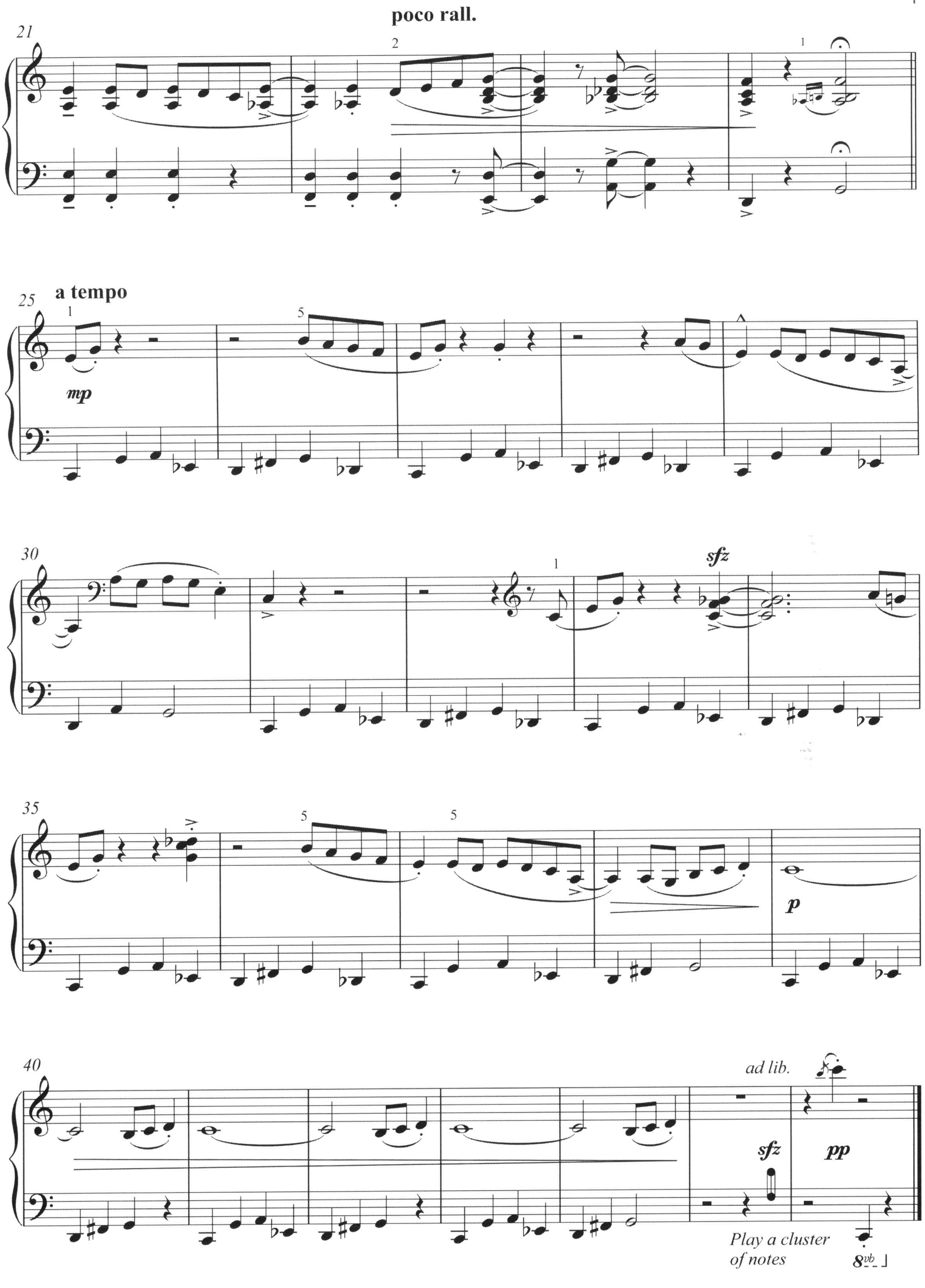

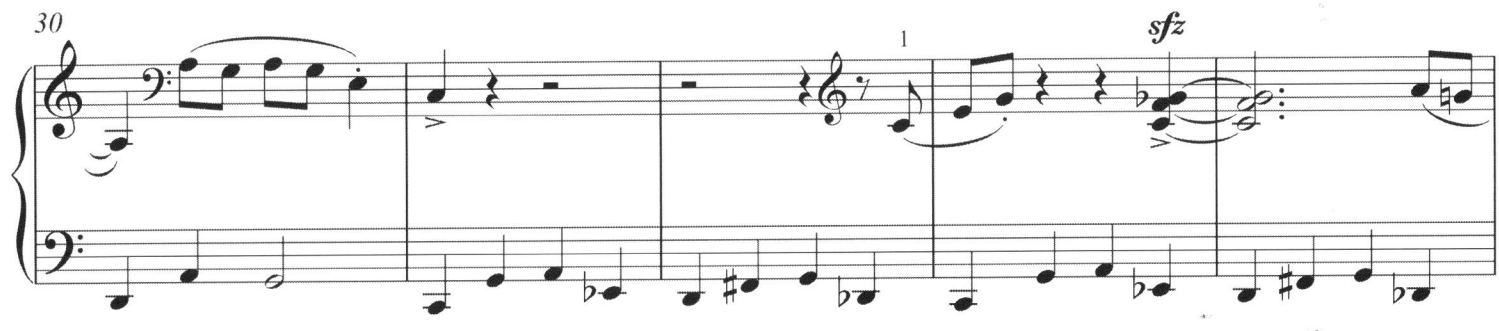

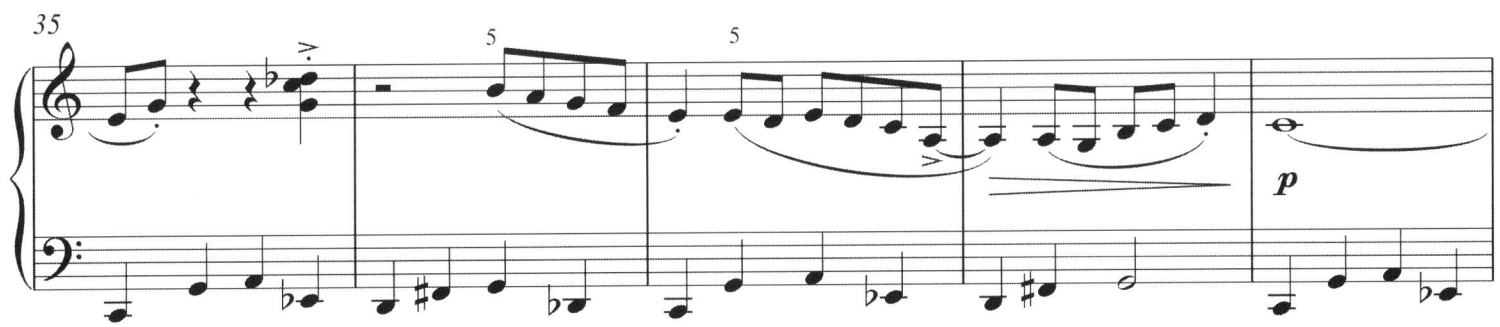

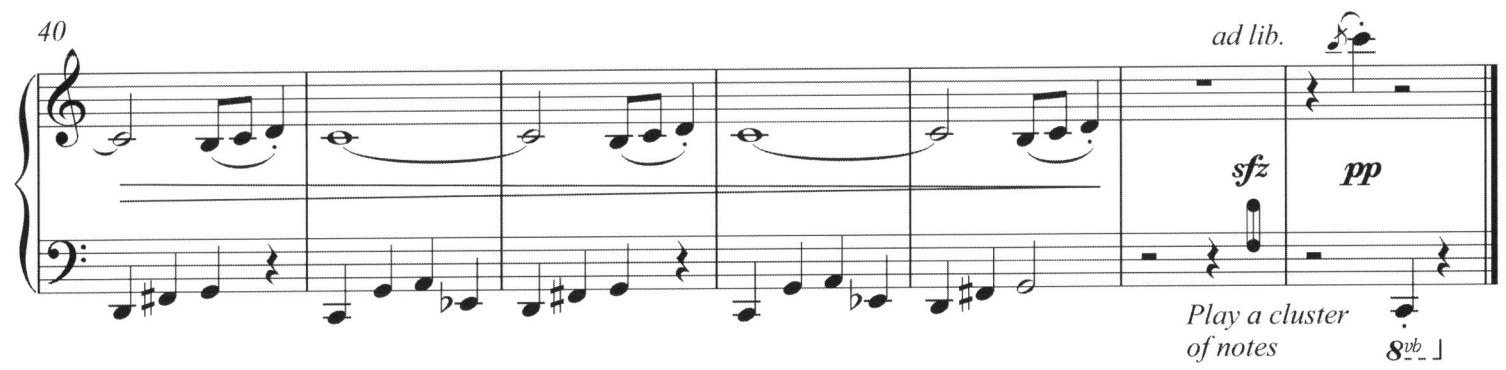

SHARK SOUP

In surfing slang, 'soup' means 'whitewater', so the title means 'whitewater full of sharks'.

Sam Wedgwood

BROWN PAPER COWBOY

Sam Wedgwood

OVER AND OVER

I'VE GOT A GROOVE

Sam Wedgwood

FOURTH STREET

Sam Wedgwood

LET THE GOOD TIMES ROLL

Sam Wedgwood

BLUE ONIONS

Sam Wedgwood